From Within Me

From Within Me

Mary L. Eaddy

Copyright © 2007 by Mary L. Eaddy.

Library of Congress Control Number: 2007902005
ISBN: Hardcover   978-1-4257-7224-6
                Softcover   978-1-4257-7207-9

All rights reserved. No part of this book may be reproduced or transmitted in any form or by any means, electronic or mechanical, including photocopying, recording, or by any information storage and retrieval system, without permission in writing from the copyright owner.

This book was printed in the United States of America.

To order additional copies of this book, contact:
Xlibris Corporation
1-888-795-4274
www.Xlibris.com
Orders@Xlibris.com
39486

Contents

1. Acknowledgments 7
2. I Am Loved! 9
3. A Great White Hope 11
4. Burst of Sun 13
5. No Good Thrills 14
6. Be Quiet, Be Still, and Listen 15
7. We Cried Yesterday, We'll Smile Tomorrow 17
8. Are You Driving on the Wrong Side of the Road? .. 18
9. Trapped in the Pit of Hell 19
10. The Buzzard 21
11. I'm Alive! 22
12. A Chance Like This Seldom Comes 23
13. A Gift of Love 25
14. Don't Judge Me 26
15. Summer School Program 27
16. Mari Hat 29
17. One Mile 30
18. A Brother's Love 31
19. Light as a Feather 32
20. The Splendor of My Garden 33
21. Place of Gloom 34
22. Who Killed the Cat? 36
23. Pink Salmons 39
24. Unpredictable 41
25. Cup 42
26. I Am Who I Am 43

27.	"Happy Birthday!"	44
28.	Birthday Cards Are Wonderful	45
29.	A Christmas Story	46
30.	A Christmas Recipe	48
31.	On My Front Lawn	50
32.	Blessings Are in This Season	51
33.	Heaven Sent	52
34.	Reasons for the Season	53
35.	Santa Can Be Spoiled Too!	54
36.	Santa Has An Angel	55
37.	When I Think about Christmas	57
38.	Just Two Things	59
39.	Peace on Earth	60
40.	Cure for Christmas	62
41.	Your Amazing Grace	64
42.	Soft White Gloves	65
43.	The People Down Below	67
44.	If I Were An Angel!	68

Acknowledgments

From Within Me is dedicated to the memories of my parents, Anna L. and Samuel W. Eaddy. I will always be grateful to them for the sacrifices they made and for placing the tools in my hands that resulted in the realization of my dream. I am grateful to God for all of the times he has manifested himself to me and to my husband, Ernest Ben, Jr., and son, A. Jerome Wallace, for their constant support and encouragement. This book has become a reality and not just a dream. I would also like to thank Virginia Pilato, Anna Esquela, Jestine Smith, Joan McCready, Mary Beth Duthoy, and Marge Penhallegon. You all believed in me so much and kept me focused on my dream. This book may not have left the comforts of home without the help of Lucille Eaddy. Thank you for your research into the publication of this book. You helped me make that leap of faith that resulted in my landing this amazing publishing company. I acknowledge Madeline Koum, Jamese Bobbitt, Linda Murel, and Toni Savoy, for their never wavering support throughout this venture, and I acknowledge Gracie Bishop, Rosalie Mobley, Beverly Eaddy, Mary Washington, Francene Bradford, Kathleen Lawson, Eleanor Kopclick, Zakia McAllison, Helen Eaddy, Barbara Ward, Alice Blackstone, Joann Ericson, Samuel Eaddy, Faith Moore, Karen Gardner, Janice Dedmond, Denise Brightful, and the photographer of Boh, Inc. located on Howard Street, Baltimore Maryland. To everyone who gave support but is not mentioned by name . . . thank you!

I Am Loved!

I am my parent's special child
I am unique in every way
I depend on what my heart has to say
And their laughter that brightened up each day
    I am Loved!

I'm self-sufficient, fresh, and alive
I have confidence in whatever I do
My independence is not based on you
I see life through my own point of view
    I am Loved!

Intellectually, my adrenalin is always high
I see the stars, each in their own space
I enjoy the sunshine that warms my face
Beneath me, I feel the earth's solid base
    I am Loved!

I have the abilities to do whatever I want
And I will allow my mind to be free
I will never cut off someone's hands to me
I'm going to be, who I was meant to be
    I am Loved!

I am gracious, smart, and articulate
I designed the mold for self-esteem
Each day I feel that I am supreme
Because I am on the winning team
      I am Loved!

I won't let my emotions lead me
Those feelings only get in my way
I set my goals high each and every day
Lord, help me to reach each one, I pray
      I am Loved!

A Great White Hope

A "Great White Hope" of future plans
A dream of fantasy
Love eternal everlasting
A foundation sure to stand

Then one day an incident
Destroyed my structure's wall
The "Great White Hope" that used to be
I stood and watched it fall

My heart was stabbed, though not by hand
Might as well have been a knife
The fault lies not in what was done
But how it came to life

I bowed my head in silent tears
My heart just bled within
Is this the price I have to pay
For an addict to be my friend?

When he's all right, the pain is gone
He claims he understand
But when the "Jones" controlled the mind
Then dope is his demand

There is still hope for the addict
Where his energy can be used
Under watchful eyes of the more matured
If their help, he don't refuse

Yes, he tore down my walls of love
And left a bitter stain
But I refuse to lose this fight
I will challenge to build again

Burst of Sun

I was a pawn in your game
A weapon in your tug of war
I felt so obsolete
Opposed to the woman you still adore

Now the war is over
I am not your pond anymore
My life has come full circle
A new knock comes to my door

I open now to a gracious smile
To my confidante and my friend
Finally, I've let the worries out
And love has entered in

He is my burst of sun in the morning
My downy late at night
I'm not sure about everything
But, I'm sure that I did this right

No Good Thrills

Every month I agonized
Over how to pay my bills
The thought haunts me every day
It brings me no good thrills

Dodging from this to pay that
Is not where I want to be
But to survive in my native land
I have to sacrifice to some degree

There is no can goods in my pantry
I do have flour to bake some bread
I can make a meal out of anything
If I stay smart and use my head

I have lard and powder milk
Sweet delights that I preserved
I made some just last night
And once again it's being served

Everyone seemed to enjoy it
At least their tummies are tight
I will not worry about tomorrow
As for now, we're full tonight

Be Quiet, Be Still, and Listen

Be quiet, be still, and listen
To what the spirit has to say
Close your mind to everything
Let your thoughts just drift away

Search your soul for an answer
Let your heart be your guide
Any problems that you may have
Just put them aside

It takes only the power of belief
And God will answer you
In his moment and his own time
He will see you through

You will have trials and tribulations
It does not mean that God doesn't care
We all have a price to pay in life
But "God's" rewards are beyond compare

He always speak, but we won't listen
He speaks in the strangest way
If we would only stop to listen
We will hear what he has to say

Sometimes when you are waiting,
He may just be waiting for you
Be quiet, be still, and listen
He will tell you what to do

We Cried Yesterday, We'll Smile Tomorrow

When each new day brings pain to life
And humming becomes a burden song
I wonder then, if nature planned
The day to "smile" prolong

Though clouds of tears dismiss the chance
To display a pleasant style
All because we missed the opportunity
Of a full wholehearted smile

The added day between the two
Was meant to judge the way
We would accept tomorrow's fate
The fate that triumphed yesterday

Blink back your tears and call it a day
Of resting from grief and sorrow
For Mother Nature no longer prolongs
We are scheduled to smile tomorrow

Are You Driving on the Wrong Side of the Road?

The traffic of life will come at you
With all of its fiery and its might
The wind will push you in the wrong lane
Without vision and/or sight

The carrier of burdens
Is headed straight to you
Look up and find your faith in God
He promised to see you through

His Son can stop incoming traffic
Demand the wind to be still
And the wind will obey his command
If it is his Father's will

He will step in and turn your life around
And lead you, while you steer
And make your destiny right again
Give you hope instead of fear

Has the wind navigated you off course
Sending you in the wrong direction?
Don't be too proud to pray for help
God's Son is your connection

Trapped in the Pit of Hell

I am trapped here in this pit of hell
The devil will not help, no matter how loud I yell
It's the most devastating place to be
I don't even think that he can find me

I look around, not a familiar face I see
All the doors are locked, and I don't have the key
I am sitting here staring, waiting for my call
Frightened and alone, with my back against the wall

If I had paint, a brush, and something to paint on
A picture of this place would surely be born
If I had these things to get through this night
What good would they be, without any light

Who is to blame for the state that I'm in?
Who led me to lose my soul to sin?
Is anyone helping me to paint this scene?
Or is everybody's life so sparkling clean?

Too late to pray and chanting doesn't ease my pain
Mama spoke of this place time and time again
But old silly me had to know the inevitable
I did not realize that life was so wonderful

I'm lost, I'm alone, I'm out of sight
I thought what I was doing was right
It's too late for a doctor; without glasses I can't see
Forgive me, I must go, the devil is calling me

The Buzzard

The buzzard search during the day
He lurks around the lame
He watches lions attack their prey
And then he steals their game

He glides through the sky with ease
His eyes absorbs the total view
And when the bloody lions run off
The buzzard does what buzzards do

He's always waiting for the kill
He helps to cleanse the earth
This all is in the cycle of things
This is taught to the buzzard since birth

Lions do the killing and they do the stealing
The buzzard never lets his guards down
And when the dead beast thumps the earth
The buzzard is always around

I'm Alive!

To slide my feet
Across a cold sheet
To fight death's angels
And defeat
    I'm Alive!

To feel the blanket
Beneath my chin
In comfort
I settled in
    I'm Alive!

To lift my legs
And the covers move
Tells me one thing
I don't have to prove
    I'm Alive!

A Chance Like This Seldom Comes

Who would have thought, this day would come
I did not have a clue
I forget that people lives can change
And a change has come for you

But what I thought, really does not matter
This was all in the Master's plan
That one day you'd travel a scenic route
Once again, giving all that you can

My prayer is for wonderful days ahead
The best is yet to come
Keep on striving toward your many goals
A chance like this seldom comes to some

I'll miss the smells of your homemade cooking
Your personality and your different styles
But most of all, your attitude
That was measured by your smiles

I'll miss your wonderful talents
The way we played Romper Room
Keep smiling, striving, and believing
And your life will surely bloom

I wish you all the best is in life
You have the class, of a fine wine
You will always be in my thoughts
And always on my mind

A Gift of Love

Marriage is a very sacred union
A complete product of God's love
This precious gift that he shares with us
Could only have come, from heaven above

Today, we toss our cares to the wind
For life can present sneaky, tempting things
But we promise to honor, love, and cherish
Our vows, marriage, and wedding rings

So, if you think, what you've seen today
Is just, maybe an illusion
Come check us out ten years from now
Then form your own conclusion
      Our marriage is a "gift of love"

Don't Judge Me

Don't judge me by my environment
As if, that is all, there is to me
I can climb the highest mountain
Or swim in the deepest sea

Like a buzzard on a funky day
I can eliminate a grave
I can pull nails from a coffin
If it's your life, I'm trying to save

Summer School Program

Summer school programs do exist
But none like Grandma Flo
It starts from morning until nightfall
And then into Saturday, her program goes

There are lessons even on Sunday
A day the kids thought they could rest
But Grandma Flo pulls off the covers
She wants her grandkids to be the best

One of the lessons that she teaches them
Is to get along and to care
To help each other, whenever they can
To be considerate and to share

Her lessons include mathematics
There is a lot of reading too
It depends on how good you are
That determines what Grandma will do

She may take them on a nature walk
To explore nature at the park
She may even take them to movies
Or keep them out until dark

But no matter what she's doing
You can best believe
The kids are always learning
Grandma always have something up her sleeve

But the rewards will be a bonus
A plus, when they return to school
They may miss a few summer activities
Like the blue waters of the swimming pool

Keep in mind that next summer is coming
This summer can't possibly last
Grandma Flo is looking forward to
Having them back, in her summer class

Mari Hat

Hi! I'm Mari Hat
Seldom I see one that I don't get
I feel it, twirl it, and pull it down on my head
I don't comb my hair; I wear a hat instead

I don't care if sweat rolls down my face
And moisten the beauty of my blouse lace
All that I know is that it must stay on
My hair is quite different, from when I was born

At times when the doorbell ring
I grab my hat and to it I cling
I tug and pull, from the bedroom, to the den
It's on real good, by the time you get in

I smile, as I greet you, because I had my way
You'll never know, what my hair's like today
That's my business; my secret; you don't need to know
About that beauty at birth, which refuses to grow

One Mile

An old man lay fast asleep
As snow fell on his head
And when the sun came to melt the snow
Everyone thought that he was dead

They removed his body from his print
And took him swiftly away
Everyone wondered what happened to him
They wondered until today

This all started on a Thursday morning
He had just come in from the cold
When he got a message from a neighbor
That his property had been sold

The old man walked for thirteen miles
He just could not understand
Why fate could have befallen him
And why he lost his land

At some point he just got tired
And laid down to rest awhile
And the worst snowfall, we ever had
Stopped his distances by one mile

A Brother's Love

A brother's love is very special
It lingers far beyond the day
When he disappeared to be with God
And his soul quietly slips away

Remember his smiles and his laughter
Reflect on the joys that you shared
Remember all of the things that he did
And your burdens, he sometimes bared

Always remember him in spirit
And sing his favorite songs
Remember the creation of a man
In your heart, where he belongs

He will not wander too far from you
He is as near as you want him to be
As he rest in the arms of Jesus
Until one day, his face, you'll see

Light as a Feather

Do not view this as a day to mourn
Instead, as a day of celebration
Appreciate those precious times
That was felt, in their generation

Speak about the love and warmth
Entertain it fondly in your mind
You only have "one chance" to love
That feeling is so hard to find

If your life has somehow been touched
By the love spread on your table
Share this love with someone else
While you're here and fully able

Create a legacy while you can
Leave special memories behind
It's never too late to love someone
Be gentle, sweet, and kind

I hope these words brings comfort
We shared many years together
And when it is your time to go
You'll fly as light as a feather

The Splendor of My Garden

I'm at home beyond my back porch
Attending to the plants in my garden
I laugh with some neighborhood kids
Who seem, not to be down hearted

Occasionally, I glance at my neighbor
As she stand watching from her door
Amazed at the sunshine and my presence
Completely astonished at my rapport

But I keep attending to my seedlings
Enjoying the sunshine that met us there
That sun which keeps my garden growing
My garden that requires tender loving care

My son brought me a new plant to wean
And I'm searching for that special place
I'll just follow the sun and its lead
And shelter my new plant in its embrace

Place of Gloom

Where is the linoleum from the floor?
Where are the curtains from the living room door?
Where are the chairs from the kitchen's table?
There is no food, but yet I hear cable

Who took the sheets from the children's bed
And left a naked mattress on the floor instead?
Where are the wash clothes to keep them clean?
Who is that person so loud and mean?

What is that foul odor in the air?
Why do kids run with their feet so bare?
Who is that drunk in the next room?
Where is the love, in a place, so gloom?

Yet you are always trying to convince me
That you are concern and that you care
Your concerns should be your children's health
And freshen the foul odor in the air

Put nice clothes on their bodies
Warm shoes on their feet
Lay them down under warm blankets,
On top a nice clean sheet

Teach them how to perform in public
And everyone will truly know
How you raise your kids at home
Because in public it will really show

Who Killed the Cat?

Was it Amy in her rage, leaving the driveway?
Was it Mammy, rushing down the stairs today?
Was it Arthur, when he fed him his last meal?
Or Martha, when he followed her to the field?

Was it Larry, while playing with his father's gun?
Or that escaped prisoner that's loose and is on the run
They have all been to my house at least once or twice
And the way they treated that cat, just was not nice

I knew that something would happen real soon
By nightfall, morning, or no later than noon
Each said that the cat was in the way
And that they would kill him, just wait, one day

When I realized that the cat was gone
He was lying stiff on the front lawn
There was blood splattered everywhere
Who ever did it, just did not care

They left it to me, to clean up the mess
And to wonder and figure, and even guess
There was even blood on the lawn moor
And the sound of a slam from the basement door

I started running and calling, but to no avail
My knees were shaking as I grabbed the rail
I pushed open the door and stepped inside
It smelt like humans who were slaughtered and died

The last time that I saw him, he was playing with my spool
As I sat knitting a sweater on a kitchen stool
He was happy and carefree and full of life
Now he lay bloodstained, from what looks like a knife

Well, it's winter, and the cat's body is gone
Even though I still visualize him on the front lawn
Lying as still as any dead thing could be
And the mystery of his death still haunts and pledges me

The basement has been washed, but does not smell clean
And the hinges of the door is on a one nail lean
The person who ran and got away
Left the odor of the bodies decay

However, yesterday I got my very first lead
As I grew more determined, it's the answer I need
I uncovered something as I was cleaning the house
A rusted knife and a bloodstained blouse

I am going crazy without an answer
To this question that's eating at me like cancer
If it was not Amy, Mammy, Arthur, or Larry
There leaves only one other person, it had to be Mary

Pink Salmons

The market has a sale on pink salmons
You can buy cans at ninety-five cents each
So, if you decide to get six cans
You'll find it's within your reach

You won't find this deal anywhere else
Not even in your neighborhood store
So, if you can afford to spend six bucks
Do it, before there is no more

I've seen how fast they are leaving
They are almost gone from the shelf
Stop thinking about what others do
Go get twenty-four cans for yourself

You can only buy six cans per visit
But it's truly worth four stops
Don't let anyone try to stop you
Except the traffic cops

And if the cops should stop you
Tell them the reason why you speed
And ask if they would let you go
Promise to reward them for their deed

Then go and get your cans of salmons
And stack them two tiers high
Make some delicious salmon patties
For the cops, when they pass by

Unpredictable

I plugged in an electric heater
To take the chill away
And when the room was warm enough
I took a bath without delay

I dried off with a soft towel
As I stepped out of the tub
Wondering if I should brush my teeth
Before I ate my grub

I glanced in the mirror
That hung fastened to the wall
Wondering how my day would be
Will there be another outside brawl

Each day is unpredictable
I never know, what I may face
So I say a prayer, before I leave
To be ready just in case

Cup

I have a special cup
It sets high up on my shelf
Every time I look at it
It reminds me of myself

Half full when I am lazy
Overflowing when I'm okay
It has a saucer when I'm sloppy
With a spoon on which to lay

I Am Who I Am

I don't have too much to give
I was not promised a lifetime to live
I don't have rubies and pearls
I am one of the natural girls

But I am "me," and there is no changing that
I can be as gentle as a kitten, or as quiet as a cat
I can be just like spoil cabbage, when not put away
Or as sly as a fox, trying to conquer his prey
     I am who I am!

"Happy Birthday!"

This is a special bundle of roses
Gathered for you from words
They have all of the fragrance of your new year
With the chirping sounds of birds

Is there anything that you will not do
To keep everything afloat
I bet you never missed a plane, a train
And never rocked a boat

If I ever needed an example
Of how busy bees can be
All anyone really has to do
Is stick with you, and they will see
      Have a restful day!

Birthday Cards Are Wonderful

Birthday cards are wonderful
And can say the sweetest thing
The covers are magnificent
Enough to make you leap and sing

However, this is not a Hallmark card
But, I've created this poem for you
It tells how much you mean to me
These words are overdue

There's no wrapping this special gift
It's already wrapped in love
And comes with the warmest wish
Under the wonderful heaven above

I wish you heartfelt moments
All through your "special" day
And that your day will end complete
With hugs, kisses, and bouquet

No pressures to disturb you
No confusion to make you sad
May each moment be full with laughter
And one of the best days, you've ever had

A Christmas Story

Chestnuts roast on an open fire
Lights blink around the window frame
Across the lawn a choir sings
In celebration of the Christ Child's name

Hot chocolate is being passed around
While the old man tells the wise men stories
Of the guiding star that led them by night
Oh yes, does this bring back memories

Ruffling noises from Christmas wrapping
Could be heard from behind a half-cracked door
Santa knows that someone's peeping
He heard their footsteps across the floor

Icicles hanging on the large pine tree
That glitters like crystals from the moonlight
We stare in awe, at the sky above
And wonder if Santa is coming tonight

Smells of pine needles, fruits, cakes, and pies
Can be smelt throughout the home
If you ever had plans to leave this place
This is one night you will not roam

Turkey is baking in the oven
Grandma is humming her favorite song
While mom sits peeling potatoes
And decides to hum along

Merry is this time and season
Smiles and laughter is everywhere
A time when family and friends come together
To show with love, they really care

Anxious, sleepy eyes are drooping
Someone falls asleep beneath the Christmas tree
While waiting for one glimpse of Santa
Wondering who this man could be

Sweet memories, we will have forever
A picture in the mind, a feeling in the heart
Christmas day won't last forever
But the spirit of Christmas will not depart

A Christmas Recipe

I came upon a recipe
It's not anything that is new
Everyone really have it
The ones who serve it are just a few

You may still have time to make it
Most of the ingredient is on your shelf
Everything that you need for this recipe
Can be found within yourself

First, you must put your heart into it
It's a Christmas recipe that's quite the dream
It includes several cups of giggles
With lots of love instead of cream

Put in some sense of humor
It is as important as a single egg
Caring will make your batter
Concern seasons like nutmeg

Shake in a generous amount of sharing
Without complaining, not one mutter
A good attitude this holiday
Should be added to replace the butter

You will also need those tears of joy
They are as exciting as vanilla extract
They will enhance the taste of your recipe
That's not a rumor, but a fact

And that dry powder, we call cinnamon
Can also be replaced too
With consideration from the heart
Which comes from inside of you

Hand mix to feel the right texture
And don't forget to taste
If you don't add enough of everything
Then this recipe will be a waste

Next, bake this in your heart of hearts
Until this mix is done
Then serve it hot this holiday
It's healthy for everyone

Now that you have this recipe
This holiday, please don't forget
To mix well, all of the ingredient
For the greatest Christmas yet

On My Front Lawn

A message blinks from my window tonight
Christmas is near, and all feels right
I'm building a huge snowman on my front lawn
The one from last year has melted and gone

I heard a car approach and slowly pass by
And a child inside let out a deep sigh
Next, I saw a turn of a head, and a big smile
A glitter in two eyes and a rise of a brow

What happened next, to my surprise
Brought joy and tears to my eyes
The kid inside admired my art
Not only that, she stole my heart

A small palm pressed the car's windowpane
As if to stop it again and again
When I realized what happened in the car
The driver had driven two blocks too far

Blessings Are in This Season

So many need us this time of year
Until, we don't know where to begin
We know it's wrong to walk away
And not let someone in

For example, the elderly, the homeless
Someone needs a nice warm bed
You'd be surprise how much it would mean
To give a sheet or a nice blanket to spread

To give a stranger a gift of love
Is more than a reality
Reach out and touch someone's heart
It will set depression free

For every struggle, there's a sacrifice
From someone just like you
Don't let this season come and go
And you did not do what you could do
      Blessings are in this Season!

Heaven Sent

With Christmas quickly approaching
We would cuddle at our parents' feet
There were pillows and blankets everywhere
These stories made Christmas Eve complete

All kinds of aroma filled the air
The smells of food, fruits, and mint
The very pines on the Christmas tree
Gave off a pleasant scent

We would glaze into their discerning eyes
As they told of their days gone by
These were fine and glorious times
Oh my, how that time did fly

Christmas time does not seem the same
Now that I am grown
The little kids around their feet
Has gone off on their own

The memories sometime linger on
I realize what my parents meant
If I only knew then, what I know now
My parents were "Heaven Sent"

Reasons for the Season

We expect so much for this holiday
More than we have ever expected before
To see people shopping, hear children laughing
The holiday's fashion hanging from every door

Snowflakes falling, people caroling
Excitement is in the air
Happy folks hugging, soft tender kissing
Poverty smothered by those who care

The thrill of dancing, the joy of romancing
Light moments everywhere
Gifts are wrapped, coats are snapping
Paper tearing, the sounds are there

There is a reason for this season
The time to show others that we care
The joy of the holiday is very special
Let's be appreciative and be aware

This holiday brings to you a cheer
May you see life differently and oh, so clear
May you be inspired and someone near
This is the "giving" time of the year
      Season's Greetings!

Santa Can Be Spoiled Too!

Santa tried to visit you last night
Of course, you were not around
Sadly, he turned and walked away
Making a sloppy, slushy, noisy sound

He walked over to his reindeer
Stroked Dasher on the face
Turning around he remembered
How he felt when he left that place

He climbed aboard his sled, "pouting"
He told the deer, "Go"
I have so many others to see
Off he went with a Ho! Ho! Ho!

The reason why I've told you this
Is because it happened to me
So, when Santa decides to visit you
In that place, arrange to be!

Santa Has An Angel

Santa was dismayed last night
His hand was as heavy as his heart
He wondered why people were so sad
And what torn their lives apart

He tinkered with some small toys
He felt that he needed to be alone
And while playing with a choo-choo train
He was disturbed by his cellular phone

Hello, Santa! I am your angel
My name is of no concern
I was sent here to deliver you
Afterward, I must return

I'm here to deliver you from sadness
And to bring back your Christmas joy
To remind you of the meaning of Christmas
You remind the old, the young, each girl and boy

I also heard that your sled needs repairing
If not, you will turn over in the sky
I cannot reveal who told me this
That's a secret between a reindeer and I

So come on, Santa, let's get started
My time here is very short
While you are checking over your list again
I'm going to give that old sled support

Santa rose from his chair, stood on his feet
What he had heard was very strange
But one thing was very clear to him
His attitude was rearranged

Santa, your sled is ready
The angel appeared once more
Only to put pep in Santa's steps
And to coach him out the door

When Santa's trips were over
And he was relaxed in his easy chair
Quietly, the angel appeared again
Hugged him, then vanished in thin air

Santa gave a hearty chuckle
As he marveled at a star above
I have been reminded of the meaning of Christmas
It really is all about "Love"

When I Think about Christmas

When I was just a little girl
My parents always filled my world
Christmas was my favorite day
Overwhelmed, I never knew what to say

The days before Christmas
We'd pick out a tree
We would all decorate it
The whole family

The night before Christmas
We'd all have our bath
This act was not science
It was strictly math

Waiting to come downstairs
Was the most fun
The small ones would walk
The oldest would run

There were bicycles, tricycles
And all sorts of toys
Anything you can image
For seven girls and five boys

There were burettes and clothes
Boots, shoes, and socks
It was really fantastic
What we found in our box

There were wagons, skates
And dolls of all kinds
When I think about Christmas
Growing up comes to mind

Just Two Things

I asked Santa for just two things
From the bag perched on his back
For Peace and Love on Christmas Day
Can you pull that from your sack?

Can you end the war that causes pain
And mend the broken heart?
Bring the love back to the land
At least that is a start

Dig deep into that bag of yours
And find a loaf of bread
Not for me to eat myself
But for a hungry one instead

Can you grab a lot of love for me
And place it in my hands?
So that I can pass it all around
To help soothe life's harsh demands

If I could have just these two things
I'd sing a song of praise
I know these gifts can help someone
Their bowed-down head to raise

Peace on Earth

Peace on earth is not the case
Joy to the world is not the same
Silent nights in the Holy Land
Gives peace on earth a brand-new name

From country to country, land to land
Peace has taken a different tone
There is turmoil at home; war abroad
And Hark the Herald may mean angels' moan

Bright flashes roaring through the sky
Is not a traditional Christmas light
Instead frequent reminders everywhere
All is not calm, and all is not bright

The clock is ticking as days go by
Yet, still there are no signs of peace
When countries can unite as friends
And selfishness, hatred, and violence cease

So when you hang your stockings
At the chimney with care
Remember the unfortunate reality
Happening to people here and everywhere

Our hands touch hearts around the world
And that feeling will come back to you
To help you through your lonely times
When your life seems grim and blue

Let the reflection in your mirror
Cause you to smile right back
You extended your hands this holiday
They were not clenched behind your back

Cure for Christmas

I felt a little under the weather
So, I went to my doctor for a cure
I explained my symptoms to him
And he helped me, I am sure

He handed me a remedy
To take three times a day
The directions printed on the label
Said, "Take straight, no other way"

He explained the affects from it
From the first dose to the last
And if I take each as prescribed
My symptoms soon would pass

Since my visit was on Christmas Eve
He encouraged me to enjoy the lights
While making my way to get into bed
To enjoy the Christmas sights

He expressed the importance of scenery
And relaxation on my way home
That the atmosphere would seem different
Like being in Paris, Italy, or Rome

With the second dose, I felt unusual
As I climbed into my gown
Remembering every word he said
I found it hard to settle down

Then, I began to sleep so peacefully
In the middle of my bed
I have to say the second dose
Went rushing to my head

The last dose I took on Christmas Day
I had the whole world to face
Even though my symptoms were gone
I took my medicine just in case

I put on my wraps and went outdoors
Just to trample through the snow
I love the cure my doctor gave
Now I take holidays nice and slow

Your Amazing Grace

Lord, thank you for your amazing grace
And for bringing us this far
For allowing us to appreciate
Your love and who we are

For lending us your listening ears
When we did not know what to do
For your love and tender mercy
We owe our thanks to you

As we enjoy the holidays
And reflect on the days gone by
We will remember what you mean to us
Through the stars twinkling in your sky

Soft White Gloves

A little boy left home one night
He packed his bag to leave
At a very tender age of ten
And sadly on Christmas Eve

All night he roamed the streets
Not sure of where to go
Frozen tears clung to his face
As he was out of food and dough

After quite a while of walking
He collapsed on one knee
And as the other touched the earth
He cried out, "Lord, help me"

Why are my parents so angry?
They used to hug me all the time
Now I don't hear I love you
These words don't cost a dime

I give up, I just don't care
I thought you were my Santa Claus
And that you could hear me pray
No matter what's the cause

As he was falling on his face
He saw a huge white glove
It caught him as he was falling
As a voice spoke words of love

Whenever you thought, I was not there
And you felt frightened and alone
Not once did I leave you
Never think that I was gone

Two gloves reached out and grabbed him
And pulled him to his chest
I understand what it is like
Let's go home, I know what's best

He lifted him up and took him home
And gently kissed him on his forehead
The next time you want to run away
Talk to your parents instead

The People Down Below

Large, fluffy, white snowflakes
Is quickly landing on the ground
Sparkling twinkles from the starlight
Dancing about without a sound

I hear a lot of steady footsteps
Crunching through the snow
People busy going here and there
Where, I do not know

I can sense that they are happy
I can tell by the chatter
Whatever in this world is happening
Only the holidays seem to matter

I realized as I drew my blinds
To the moon and all of its glow
I'll always have this memory
Because of the people down below

If I Were An Angel!

If I were an angel
I'd turn your gray skies blue
You would always feel my presence
And my soft wings wrapped around you

I'd fly high and hang a star
On top of your Christmas tree
Come down and fly around it
Placing lights for all to see

Beneath it would be the biggest gift
Without paper or a bow
And each of you can share it
You can't wrap love . . . Didn't you know!

But, I am not an angel
Equipped with wings to fly
Nor can I be everywhere you are
Or change God's perfect sky

The gift of love, I have to give
And to all of you, I want to share
This precious gift God gave to me
It will go with you everywhere